# Uncle Terry's Glasses

**David Rish**

Illustrated by Jeff Lang

# Contents

# Chapter 1

# **Winter Vacation**

Olivia could see the snow-covered airport from her seat on the plane. Workers were shoveling something white onto the runway.

"What are they doing, Mom?" Olivia asked, pointing to the workers.

"They're spreading salt. It helps melt the snow and ice so that we can land safely," Mom explained.

The plane touched down and Olivia grinned. She was excited about spending winter vacation at her cousins' farm.

Uncle Terry, Aunt Gillian, and Olivia's cousins, Simone and Rick, greeted Olivia and her mom at the airport.

"Welcome to winter!" said Simone. "The pond behind our house is completely frozen."

"We can go skating on it," said Rick. "The ice is nice and thick."

Olivia couldn't wait!

"Let's get going," Aunt Gillian said. "There's a warm home-made apple pie waiting in our kitchen."

"Yum!" said the three cousins together.

ARRIVALS

# Chapter 2

# Stuck in Ice

Right after finishing their pie, the cousins put on their coats, hats, and gloves and headed outside to the pond. The sun was shining, making the snow sparkle.

At the pond, they put on their skates and went out onto the ice. Olivia had skated only a few times before, so she was a little wobbly. It was hard to stay on her feet and not fall down!

Getting to her feet after yet another fall, Olivia noticed something trapped just beneath the ice's surface. It looked like it was caught in the leaves of some water weeds.

"Look!" Olivia said to her cousins. "It looks like there's a pair of eyeglasses stuck in the ice!"

"Those look like Dad's reading glasses!" Simone said. "Rick, remember when he helped that calf that was stuck in the mud last fall? He couldn't find his glasses afterward."

"They must have fallen into the pond and got frozen when winter came," said Rick.

"Do you think we can get Uncle Terry's glasses back for him?" asked Olivia, scratching the ice with her skate. The ice was very hard and thick.

"Let's leave Dad's glasses right where they are," Rick said with a laugh. "If he doesn't have them, he won't be able to read my report card!"

"But he keeps running into walls and bumping his nose, poor Dad," Simone said.

Olivia knew her cousins were joking. She grinned at them.

## Chapter 3

# Finding a Solution

The cousins tried to think of ways to rescue Uncle Terry's glasses.

"Let's break the ice with something hard, like a hammer," said Olivia.

"We might break Dad's glasses," Simone said. "And the fish might be scared by the movement and the noise."

"Are there fish swimming under the ice?" Olivia asked, looking surprised.

"Yes—there's still enough oxygen in the water for them to breathe," Simone said.

"I didn't know that," Olivia said.

"I have an idea!" Rick said suddenly. "We need heat. Watch this." He pulled off his glove. Snowflakes landed on his hand. Because of the heat of his body, they quickly melted.

"We need a giant magnifying glass," Rick continued. "We could catch the sunlight with the glass and use it to melt the ice."

Just then, Aunt Gillian came outside with mugs of hot chocolate and marshmallows.

"Mmm! Thanks, Mom," said Simone.

"Thanks, Aunt Gillian," said Olivia.

"Excellent!" said Rick.

Olivia showed Aunt Gillian Uncle Terry's glasses trapped under the ice.

"We're trying to think of ways to get them out," she said.

"I've got another idea!" said Rick.

He tipped some of his hot drink onto the ice. But the ice didn't melt. The hot chocolate froze instead.

"Chocolate ice cream, yum," said Rick, picking up some of the slushy chocolate with his fingers.

"Boys!" said Simone, rolling her eyes at Olivia.

Chapter 4

# Olivia's Idea

Soon it was time for lunch. Uncle Terry had made hamburgers and a salad. Everything was delicious, and Olivia was hungry after her morning of skating with her cousins.

As she started to eat her burger, Olivia noticed the salt shaker on the table. She suddenly remembered landing at the airport that morning.

She had an idea.

"Maybe we can try to melt the ice with salt," she exclaimed. "Just like they were doing at the airport this morning."

"That's right," said Olivia's mom. "The workers at the airport did that so the plane could land safely."

Everyone agreed that using salt to melt the ice was worth a try.

Uncle Terry gave the cousins a big box of salt that he used to melt the ice on the sidewalk and driveway.

After lunch, the cousins headed out to the pond again.

## Chapter 5

# Cool Glasses!

Olivia poured some salt on the ice where the glasses were trapped.

"The ice on the pond is really thick," said Olivia. "But we're in luck—Uncle Terry's glasses are close to the surface."

"You're right, only the top layer has to melt," said Simone.

All three cousins watched hopefully.

"Look!" said Rick. "Something is happening. But I think it's going to take a while."

The cousins went back to skating. Olivia was getting much better on her skates. She hardly fell over at all anymore.

Now and again, the cousins checked to see if the ice was still melting. Finally, late in the afternoon, they were able to scrape away a small pile of slush.

Rick reached down and gently pulled his
dad's glasses from the slush and the
pieces of ice and water weeds.

"Hurray, we did it!"
the cousins cried.

Rick tried on his dad's glasses.

"I never realized Dad wore 'cool' glasses," he joked as his hot breath fogged up the lenses.

Just then, Uncle Terry came outside.

"You did it! You rescued my glasses!
Well done, kids!" he said.

A few days later, it was time for Olivia and her mom to go home.

"You'll have to come back for summer vacation, Olivia," Rick said.

"We'll be able to take a rowboat out on the pond then," said Simone.

Olivia grinned. "I can hardly wait!"

## Water Into Ice

Water changes state from a liquid to a solid (ice) when the temperature of the water falls and stays below the freezing point. Ice thickens throughout the winter months and then melts as air and water temperatures warm in the spring.

Large ponds, or lakes, freeze from the shore to the middle. Ponds also freeze from the top down—but usually not all the way to the bottom. Fish do not freeze when the surface of a pond freezes.

The freezing point of water is 32° Fahrenheit (32°F), or 0° Celsius (0°C).

## Think About the Story

In *Uncle Terry's Glasses*, cousins skating on a pond find a special surprise—Uncle Terry's glasses frozen in the ice! Think about these questions.

- How did Uncle Terry's glasses become stuck in the pond?
- How do the cousins remove the glasses from the ice?
- What will happen to the pond in the spring? How does the pond change during the year?

To learn more about water and other kinds of matter, read the books below.

**SUGGESTED READING**
**Windows on Literacy**
*Water Can Change*
*Everything Is Made of Matter*

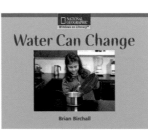